JESUS

and the gift of

FRIENDSHIP

WRITTEN BY

Trillia Newbell

ILLUSTRATED BY

Kristen & Kevin Howdeshell

CROSSWAY

WHEATON, ILLINOIS

Jesus and the Gift of Friendship

Copyright © 2023 by Trillia J. Newbell

Illustrations © 2023 Crossway

Published by Crossway
    1300 Crescent Street
    Wheaton, Illinois 60187

Illustrations, book design, and cover design: Kristen & Kevin Howdeshell

First printing 2023

Printed in China

ISBN: 978-1-4335-8548-7

Library of Congress Cataloging-in-Publication Data
Names: Newbell, Trillia J., author. | Howdeshell, Kristen, illustrator. | Howdeshell, Kevin, illustrator.
Title: Jesus and the gift of friendship / Trillia Newbell ; illustrated by Kristen and Kevin Howdeshell.
Description: Wheaton, Illinois : Crossway, 2023. | Audience: Ages 3–6
Identifiers: LCCN 2022040561 | ISBN 9781433585487
Subjects: LCSH: Jesus Christ—Juvenile fiction. | Friendship—Juvenile fiction.
Classification: LCC BT302 .N49 2023 | DDC 232.9/01—dc23/eng/20230313
LC record available at https://lccn.loc.gov/2022040561

Crossway is a publishing ministry of Good News Publishers.

RRDS   33   32   31   30   29   28   27   26   25   24   23
15   14   13   12   11   10   9   8   7   6   5   4   3   2   1

"You are my friends if you
do what I command you."
John 15:14

Zeke loved to play outside. He splashed in puddles. He skipped and jumped and made mud pies. Every day he played outside with his best friend, Sam. Sam sometimes threw mud at Zeke, but Zeke didn't mind. He loved to play with his friend Sam.

But one day Zeke got the news that he would soon pack all of his things into boxes and suitcases and move miles and miles away from Sam. Zeke was sad.

Every day he jumped and played, hoping he would not move away. But on a sunny summer day, a big truck parked in front of his home and filled up quickly with everything they owned.

Zeke was very sad.

After the truck pulled up to his new home, Zeke pushed through the piles of boxes to unpack all of his toys.

That morning there had been a strong rainstorm so the ground was perfect for mud pies.

As he dug and dug and plopped the pile of mushy brown soil into a big mound, he thought of Sam. Boy, did he wish Sam could play with him.

Zeke played in the mud all summer long. Every time he played, he wished Sam could play with him.

One bright sunny day, Zeke felt sad. Although he loved to play and splash in puddles, he didn't want to play alone. Zeke got brave and asked his mom if he could find a friend. She took his hand and walked outside. "Oh look," she said, "there's a new kid outside. Let's ask if he can play."

Zeke remembered that a family had just moved in next door. Would the boy next door be the friend who would play and explore? Zeke was so excited and couldn't wait anymore. He shouted out,

WILL YOU BE MY FRIEND?!?!?!

The new kid was surprised and didn't seem sure, so he ran into his house.

Zeke looked at his mom with tears in his eyes.

"Will I ever find a friend?"

Zeke's mom touched his shoulder and, looking into his big brown eyes, she said,

"Friendships take time. Let's try again tomorrow."

Tomorrow came and the next day and the next day, and Zeke still did not have a friend. One day when Zeke was feeling extra lonely, his mom told him good news. "Zeke," she said, "you do have a friend. His name is Jesus."

Zeke was a bit confused and asked, "What do you mean?"
He had read about Jesus and all of his miracles but had
never considered him his friend.

His mom explained, "Jesus is the Son of God, the great high priest, the Savior of the world! Did you also know that when Jesus was here on earth he had friends?

"And Jesus made friends with all sorts of people. Everyone Jesus interacted with was different from him. Would you like to hear about some of his friends?" she asked.

Zeke wanted to hear all about Jesus's friends. Sitting in his mother's lap, he listened as she began to tell of all the people Jesus met.

"Jesus made friends in many places. One day while walking by a big sea, Jesus saw two brothers fishing. The brothers were named Peter and Andrew. Peter and Andrew had big nets to catch fish for the day. They were likely going to sell the fish. Jesus asked the two brothers to join him on his journey. Do you know what they did? They dropped everything right there and followed him!

"Jesus found other friends to take long journeys with him too, like Matthew the moneyman and Simon the rebel. His friends were called disciples, and they shared the good news that anyone who believed in Jesus could be his friend too.

"Jesus made friends with different people. He made friends with people from foreign lands and people who worked for the government. Jesus made friends with those who were very sick and people who had lots of wealth. Jesus made friends with men and women and grandmothers and grandfathers. Jesus loved children, like you, and made friends with them too.

"Because Jesus is your friend, you can tell him anything.

"You can tell him when you are sad.

"You can tell him when you are happy.

"And because Jesus is a friend, you can ask him for anything.

"Do you want another friend?

"Ask Jesus.

"Jesus doesn't always give us what we want but we can always ask. He will give us what we need."

That night, Zeke got on his knees and prayed, "Jesus, thank you for being my friend. Would you please give me another friend, like Sam? Amen."

From then on, every morning Zeke would run outside and wait for a friend. He waited and waited and waited. The leaves turned orange and fell off the trees. Snow came and covered the ground. Birds began to chirp, and then came April showers.

A year went by and Zeke still did not have a friend in his neighborhood.

Every night he still prayed, "Jesus, thank you for being my friend.

"Would you please give me another friend, like Sam?"

One sunny day, Zeke went outside just like he always did. He dug and dug and plopped the pile of mushy brown soil into a big mound, and he thought of Sam. A girl with coily, curly hair came bopping down the

"Hey, what's your name?" she asked.

"Zeke," he yelled out. "What's your name?"

"My name is Gabby. Would you like to play, Zeke?" she asked.

Zeke thought about his prayer. Every night for months, Zeke had asked Jesus for a friend like Sam. Gabby was tall for her age and slender. She had milky brown skin and freckles all over. Gabby wasn't anything like Sam.

Zeke looked up with his big brown eyes and said, "Yes, I'd love to play. Do you like mud pies?"

Zeke and Gabby made mud pies all afternoon.

She taught Zeke how to play hopscotch too. All summer long they played and played.

They had so much fun!

As Zeke was getting ready for bed one fall evening, he remembered his mom's story about Jesus and all of Jesus's friends. Jesus had friends like Sam and like Gabby. He had friends like Zeke too. Jesus had all sorts of friends, Zeke remembered. With a big grin on his face, he ran and got his mom.

"Mom, Mom!" he exclaimed. "Jesus answered my prayer! Now I have all sorts of friends! I have Sam and I have Gabby, just like Jesus!"

His mom grinned back and said, "Yes, my son, Jesus wants us to be just like him and have all sorts of friends."

That night, Zeke prayed, "Jesus, thank you for being my friend.

"And thank you for giving me friends like Sam and Gabby.

"Please help me be a good friend to them, and I pray you'll give me more friends, just like you gave me Sam and Gabby."

Note to Parents

Often, children (and adults!) need to be reminded about who Jesus is. It's easy to forget that the one who died on a cross, bearing the wrath that we deserve, and who lives as the risen King is also the one who calls us his friends.

Jesus told his disciples that they were no longer servants; they were his friends (John 15:15). Jesus tells us that if we do what he commands, we too are his friends (v. 14). What an awesome privilege to be a friend of the great high priest! We have an intimate relationship with the Lord. We can relate to him as our Savior and our friend.

Jesus and the Gift of Friendship helps kids and adults alike understand this glorious truth. We have a friend in Jesus. Life is hard and lonely, so we can pray with our children, asking our friend to be with us just as Zeke did. God says that he draws near to us in our loneliness (Ps. 145:18; Heb. 4:16). As parents, following the example of Zeke's mother, we can help our kids know our friend. And because Jesus is our friend, we can also ask him for all things. Kids can begin to build the muscle of running to the Lord in prayer for everything, including the precious request for a new friend. So on bended knee, let's go to our Lord and friend, and ask him for all we need. Like Zeke, we might even find that God has something in mind for us that we'd never think to ask or imagine.